Daily Bread

Devotional Readings
From the Members of
True Love Church of Refuge

Delisa Lindsey, Chief Editor

The Holy Bible, New Living Translation, copyright ©1996, 2004, 2007. Used by permission of Tyndale House Publishers, Inc., Carol Stream, Illinois 60188.

GOD'S WORD is a copyrighted work of God's Word to the Nations. Quotations are used by permission. Copyright 1995 by God's Word to the Nations. All rights reserved.

"Scripture quotations are from the ESV® Bible (The Holy Bible, English Standard Version®), copyright © 2001 by Crossway, a publishing ministry of Good News Publishers. Used by permission. All rights reserved."

Unless otherwise stated, all Scripture Quotations taken from the King James Version of the Holy Bible. All Rights Reserved.

Published by
It's All About Him Media & Publishing
A Multimedia Division of True Love Church of Refuge
5201-D Nations Ford Road
Charlotte, NC 28217
www.truelovechurchofrefuge.org
www.aahmp.weebly.com
www.facebook.com/ItsAllAboutHimMediaPublishing
980-522-8096

Chief Editor and Cover Design
Delisa Lindsey

Churches and organizations, order your own set of personalized devotionals, contact the IAHMP office a 980-522-8096. Ghost writing services available.

Daily Love

DEDICATION

To the friends and family of True Love Church of Refuge, we thought you might appreciate this token of our love toward you for worshipping with us. Your spiritual growth and Godly success means a lot to us so much so that we put together this devotional to keep you encouraged and inspired along your Christian journey. May our gift to you bless you and keep you in the love of God.

If you are ever in the need of prayer, please don't hesitate to reach out to us. Our contact information is:

True Love Church of Refuge
5201-D Nations Ford Road
Charlotte, NC 28217
980-522-8096
www.truelovechurchofrefuge.org
Visit us on Facebook

We love you with the love of Jesus,

True Love Church of Refuge Family

Daily Love

Special Thanks

We give God all the highest praise and honor for all things. This book ministry would not have been possible without Him. We are grateful to God for the spiritual leadership at True Love Church of Refuge. We bless God for our overseers, Apostle John and Prophet Delisa Lindsey. We are thankful for our Pastor, Yvonne Williams and the entire ministry staff at True Love.

This devotional is a compilation of teachings, messages of hope, testimonies, and verses of encouragement. We acknowledge our own in house publisher, It's All About Him Media & Publishing and our Editor, Delisa Lindsey. We thank Maritza Griffith for assisting with the gathering of material for this book. We thank Latricia Henry for naming this project, Daily Love. And we are so honored to mention our contributing authors; Tystatian Holloway, Yvonne Williams, Virginia Holt, Jennifer Robinson, Shelia Johnson, Marva Roseborough, Avery Ascue, Delisa Lindsey, and John Lindsey.

May the Lord bless, keep, and strengthen you for the journeys ahead in Jesus name. Amen.

Daily Love

The Lord is My Shepherd

The Lord is my shepherd; I shall not want.

He maketh me to lie down in green pastures:
he leadeth me beside the still waters.

He restoreth my soul: he leadeth me in the
paths of righteousness for his name's sake.

Yea, though I walk through the valley of the
shadow of death, I will fear no evil: for thou
art with me; thy rod and thy staff they
comfort me.

Thou preparest a table before me in the
presence of mine enemies: thou anointest
my head with oil; my cup runneth over.

Surely goodness and mercy shall follow me
all the days of my life: and I will dwell in the
house of the Lord for ever.

The Lord's Prayer

After this manner therefore pray ye:

Our Father which art in heaven,
Hallowed be thy name.

Thy kingdom come, Thy will be done in
earth, as it is in heaven.

Give us this day our daily bread.

And forgive us our debts, as we forgive
our debtors.

And lead us not into temptation, but
deliver us from evil: For thine is the
kingdom, and the power, and the glory,
for ever. Amen.

FAITH

STILL I RISE

Life has its way of knocking you down and throwing you for some loops. The path of life is filled with ups and downs and highs and lows. You may even had some dead situations like Lazarus' in John 11:21-23, "Then said Martha unto Jesus, Lord, if thou hadst been here, my brother had not died. But I know, that even now, whatsoever thou wilt ask of God, God will give it thee. Jesus saith unto her, Thy brother shall rise again." Nobody said this way would be easy. Even Jesus said that in the world you will have tribulation. But He also said, "Be of good cheer". Cheer means happy and optimistic. "I have overcome", and if He has overcome, then what does that make us? You are more than a conqueror. John 16:33, "These things I have spoken unto you, that in me ye might have peace. In the world ye shall have tribulation: but be of good cheer; I have overcome the world."

I believe that God wants His people to take courage. No matter where you are or what you may be going through at this point in life, I am here to let you know that you will rise again. Some of you have had a long, hard journey in this Christian way.

Things have not been as easy as you may have thought it would have been. Remember when you first were saved and you had an invincibility about you? Remember saying, "I love the Lord", and "I will die for the Lord." "I am going to preach. I am going to have a big ministry." Consider the words of Peter in John 13:36-37, "Simon Peter said unto him, Lord, whither goest thou? Jesus answered him, Whither I go, thou canst not follow me now; but thou shalt follow me afterwards. Peter said unto him, Lord, why cannot I follow thee now? I will lay down my life for thy sake." We were sometimes blinded by zeal. But when you get past talking the talk and start walking the walk, you started asking yourself, 'What's going on?" What's happening? Where did this come from? Satan knows the real. He knows who is pretending.

When things begin to change and you then realize that religion can't save you, know that the heat has been turned on. Only those who are caught up in relationship with God will stand. Religion sets you up high and allows you to fall hard but I am standing on a relationship with God in power and so should you.

I am here to tell you that you will rise above it all. Some of you have been let down by those who were close to you who said they had your best interest at heart but God says, "You will rise above it all". How many of you have been rewarded evil for good and it seems like all of your labor is in vain? There is coming a day for you that God will lift up the heads of your enemies upon the gallows. Esther 7:10, "So they hanged Haman on the gallows that he had prepared for Mordecai. Then was the king's wrath pacified." You shall rise again. We have been up and down and going through for the Kingdom of God's sake. We have been slain and crucified on every side but God wants you to know that you will rise above it all.

There is coming a tipping point where God is going to vindicate His people. God is declaring the storms over for some of you. He is encouraging some of you through the storm. For some, the famine is over. For some, the breakthrough is at the door along with your miracle and the healing that you've been waiting on. Some of you are about to experience a place in God that you have never known because He is drawing you. You are in a place of alignment. Ps. 102:13, "Thou shalt arise, and have mercy upon Zion: for the time to favour her, yea, the set time, is come." The hunger is there and the time is right. Payday is coming after a-while. You are coming out of your evening and joy is coming in your morning. It doesn't matter where you are or what it looks like for you right now, don't give up. Pick your head up. You are a king. You can't keep a good man down. You shall rise again. In Jesus name, stand up.

I declare and decree that this people shall rise up and take their places as kings and priests. These shall rise and not fall. They shall rise and prosper. They shall rise in victory. They shall rise in favor. They shall rise to any and every challenge that this world or their enemies shall present them and they shall overcome. They shall rise in business, in ministry, as successful parents, and successful spouses. They shall rise. I say to you, "Arise."

John Lindsey

So then faith cometh by hearing, and hearing by the word of God.

Romans 10:17

PATIENCE

Patience is a virtue we all need. With it, we have the ability to wait on the Lord to give us instruction in areas of our life where it is most needed. Many a foolish man have made life altering decisions in the heat of the moment when their emotions were under attack. We need to realize that certain choices cannot be undone. Some of those outcomes will haunt us until the day we depart this life.

Isaiah 40:31, "Yet those who wait for the LORD Will gain new strength; They will mount up with wings like eagles, They will run and not get tired, They will walk and not become weary."

Patience will teach you how to cope with uneasy and difficult conditions until the time comes for change. It will empower you and grant you the strength you need in the face of turmoil to stand your ground and maintain your integrity. Patience is a necessity for the believer because there are certain issues in our personal life that WILL NOT change overnight. We will need the graces of patience to sustain us in those most challenging times when we need to put our trust in Almighty God.

James 1:19-20, "This you know, my beloved brethren. But let everyone be quick to hear, slow to speak and slow to anger; for the anger of man does not achieve the righteousness of God."

A hasty man is a foolish man. They will always make impetuous decisions and act out of their emotions. An impatient person hardly sees the righteousness of God working on their behalf because they lack the stamina to wait until He does so. A patient man does not have to answer every call, respond to every matter, or involve himself in everything. He understands that one word said or deed done out of season can invoke a domino effect that can set off circumstances and spin them out of our control.

Wikipedia defines patience as, "The state of endurance under difficult circumstances, which can mean persevering in the face of delay or provocation without acting on annoyance/anger in a negative way; or exhibiting forbearance when under strain, especially when faced with longer-term difficulties. Patience is the level of endurance one can take before negativity. It is also used to refer to the character trait of being steadfast. Antonyms include hastiness and impetuousness."

Ephesians 4:1-2, "I, therefore, the prisoner of the Lord, entreat you to walk in a manner worthy of the calling with which you have been called, with all humility and gentleness, with patience, showing forbearance to one another in love."

The Lord is calling us to patience. He desires us to wait on Him for instruction before we say or do certain things that may bring added grief to our own lives. Many a man have suffered for making impulsive decisions and some have even caused their own departure from this life because they could not endure their difficulties. Teach us Lord how to wait.

Psalm 37:7-9, "Rest in the LORD and wait patiently for Him; Do not fret because of him who prospers in his way, Because of the man who carries out wicked schemes. Cease from anger, and forsake wrath; Do not fret, it leads only to evildoing. For evildoers will be cut off, But those who wait for the LORD, they will inherit the land."

Delisa Lindsey

But without faith it is impossible to please him: for he that cometh to God must believe that he is, and that he is a rewarder of them that diligently seek him.

Hebrews 11:6

IF GOD WERE TO STRIP YOU OF YOUR BLESSING WOULD YOU STILL BLESS HIM?

It is so easy to bless God when everything is on the up and up but would you still bless God even if He took away the blessings? Job walked upright before God and was very blessed but there came a time when God wanted to prove Himself on Job's behalf. The Lord loosed a whirlwind of tests upon him, stripping away practically everything he had. When Job tore his mantle and fell down and worshipped God in tears, the tears confirmed that God stripped some very important things and people from Job's life.

In the midst of all this, Job still had the mindset to worship God. Even with a whirlwind of storms spewing around him, he did not let his circumstances push him away from the Lord. Job took advantage of the moment and let it guide him closer to God. Many of us in the Body of Christ would have been pouring sweat as soon as the first hell hound was loosed in our life which brings me to my next question...

Are we really as strong in the faith as we say we are? To those who automatically said, "Yes", I ask you this, "Are you sure?" The funny thing about this is God has a way of showing us who we really are in the midst of our trials and how much of Him is actually in us.

If you pay close attention spiritually, you would realize that during Job's trials, God was deconstructing and reconstructing him for the glory of God. This had nothing to do with Job walking in unrighteousness. The Bible states in Job 1:1 that he walked upright before the Lord. God had it in His mind that He loved Job so much that He just wanted to bless Job more than he could even imagine. Job had to go through for the breakthrough. All of Job's suffering was not in vain. God had a perfect plan for his life as He does for you and me.

One thing I find interesting is that, in the middle of your test, if satan can't get to you one way, he will use any and everything else, even people. Yes it could be your spouse or your friend. Do not be surprised. Job's wife spoke a very foolish thing and Job quickly rebuked her for being a willing vessel for satan. This brings me to my next question.

When satan shows up, no matter what the situation is, would you rebuke him or salute him? When I say salute him I mean pull up a chair and commune in his foolery. Some of us choose to commune with satan out of fear when God has not given us the spirit of fear but of love, power, and a sound mind. One example of being fearful is being afraid to just flat out tell the enemy, "NO", and that can be towards anything he says. The enemy loves manipulating those who carry fearful spirits because he can use them as puppets.

In conclusion, we must bless God with or without a blessing because He deserves all the glory for He is good. Any trace of fear in our lives must be broken in order to move forward.

Tystaytian C. Holloway

Trust in the LORD with all thine heart; and lean not unto thine own understanding.

Proverbs 3:5

NO TURNING BACK

Once upon a time I had a dream. In that dream I was taking care of some business at a building. When I completed my business, I left and just as I crossed the street I remembered something else that I needed. I turned to go back to the building and was immediately facing a concrete barrier. I could see over the barrier but I couldn't get back to the building. The entire street was gone. The building was still in view but there was no access to get to it. I awakened and asked the Lord what was He saying? He reminded me of the story of Lot's wife (Genesis 19).

As Lot and his family were leaving Sodom, they were instructed to not look back but Lot's wife couldn't resist. She looked back and turned into a pillar of salt. She looked back and became stuck right there; couldn't move another inch. She had a love for the things of the world and when given a chance to move forward and not look back, she was disobedient. There is nothing in our past that we need when God is launching us forward. He says, "No turning back." That means no turning back to past sins, no turning back to familiar habits, no turning back to familiar sermons, familiar places, familiar ministry assignments, or familiar friends but embrace the "new" of what He's doing in your life.

"Therefore if any man be in Christ, he is a new creature: old things are passed away; behold all things are become new". (2 Cor. 5:17 KJV). There is nothing we need from the past. There is nothing we need from "back there". God has provided everything we need for where we are going. (Philippians 4:19).

When faced with those "concrete barriers" called life, whether it's financial problems, evictions, repossessions, homelessness, unemployment, illness, divorce, loss of a loved one, loneliness, friends turning their backs, fear, or whatever that "concrete barrier" is, do not allow it to move you out of position. Don't turn back – don't get stuck on what has been but keep moving forward. God has a plan and purpose for your life according to His word in Jeremiah 29:11. Be encouraged and know that your future is bright. God wants to take you to another level in Him. Receive it in the name of Jesus.

Marva Roseborough

For I know the thoughts that I think toward you, saith the LORD, thoughts of peace, and not of evil, to give you an expected end.

Jeremiah 29:11

MY LIFE HAS CHANGED

I was on the road to destruction living a lifestyle that involved me selling and using drugs, being raped, and facing death. It was at this point that I decided I needed a change. I knew that God had something better for me. This, however, would be by far my biggest decision and challenge I would ever face.

Growing up, I was surrounded by family and so called friends who were drug dealers. Before there were blunts there was the EZ-wider. I could remember times when my God-mother would take me to New York to pick up marijuana every Friday night. When we returned home, she would separate the seeds from the weed. Using rolling paper, she would roll up at least a hundred joints and instructed me to sell them at school for $5 each. Hence, at the age of 14, I had become a drug dealer. I made a lot of money from selling marijuana and I enjoyed the fast pace of money flowing through my hands. At age 16, the streets became my teacher, not school, and I began selling rock cocaine. I became a user by the time I was 21 years old and it was that point that I fell deep into the slipping away of my life.

By the time I had reached 30, I had been raped at gun point and with a knife. In 2002, I was arrested for assault which landed me in a place where I was continually surrounded by convicts, murderers, child abusers, and drug dealers. Prison was totally different from the streets because I had no freedom. I had to share a room with people I hardly knew. The door is shut at certain hours of the day and if you're lucky, you might come across someone you know. It was there in prison that my life started to turn on its axels.

I had been locked up for 10 months and began to get comfortable with my environment. One Sunday morning, I decided to go to church with a few of my fellow inmates. The service was very enlightening and inspired me. Since that day, I felt the urgency to learn more about the man named, Jesus Christ. I would read and pray every day and on the 19th day, I was released from prison both physically and mentally.

When I returned home, my cousin, Timothy, invited me to Pastor Thurman Evans' church in Linden, NJ. It was then that I fell in love with Jesus and became zealous for the Word of God. Every time I would read, God spoke. Every time I didn't understand, He would give me clarity. The Word of God became my instructions for life and living the Word of God ordered my footsteps towards my deliverance.

When I gave my life to Christ, I had more respect for myself. Many years have passed since then and I am still living and standing on every Word of God. I'm able to share with others my life's experience of the streets and the goodness of God. He has done a lot for me, so I love to share His goodness with mankind. Eventually, I relocated to a new state where there were unfamiliar faces. God surrounded me with people who had positive energy, kindness, better guidance, and the right connections.

In 2006, I walked the stage of victory receiving my high school diploma. Furthering my education, I now have 3 years experience of college on my plate and am still enrolled. I'm covered by positive people. I have a healthy relationship with God and my Christian brothers and sisters. I noticed that people would come over to my house for prayer and that I became a magnet for children. I began writing spiritual poems and giving them out at God's request. Back home, a lot of people who knew me didn't accept nor respect me anymore. There were familiar with the old me and couldn't comprehend the new me. However, God would remind me from time to time that He is doing a new thing and He taught me to close my ears to negativity.

Finally, my life as I would know it has changed and on this road I learned to shun my past that was leading me to destruction and to embrace my future.

Sheila Johnson

Cast thy burden upon the LORD, and he shall sustain thee: he shall never suffer the righteous to be moved.

Psalm 55:22

THUS SAYS THE LORD, I AM.......
KNOW WHO YOU ARE

Thus says the Lord, "I am made in the image of God." (Gen. 1:27). To be made in the image of God means that I possess the same attributes of God. Not in that I'm equal with God because He is all knowing and present everywhere (I am not), but I have His nature of love and compassion. I have His nature of mercy. God is light and He created us to be a light. (Matt 5:14-16). I am holy (1 Peter 1:16). I am righteous. I am faithful, I am wise, and knowledgeable. I am fearfully and wonderfully made; how can I not be? Because thus says the Lord, "I am made in His image."

Thus says the Lord, "I am His child" (1 John 3:1). I have been adopted into the family of Christ (Eph.1:5). I am an heir and therefore entitled to every spiritual inheritance. Because I am His child, He has anointed me with gifts. I am a carrier of the anointing of God. I am a citizen of the Kingdom of God. I am His chosen vessel.

Thus says the Lord, "I am a new creature in Christ". I am free from the bondage of sin. I have been redeemed. I am justified. My body is the temple of the Holy Spirit that dwells in me. I have the power to overcome every snare that has been set before me. I am a soldier. I am His spokesperson. I am His evangelist. I have the mind of Christ to do the will of the Father. I am bold and confident to proclaim the Gospel of Jesus Christ. I am His administrator. I am a witness for Christ in the earth. Thus says the Lord, "I am that I am". Hallelujah.

Marva Roseborough

HOLY SPIRIT

WHO IS HOLY SPIRIT?

The Holy Spirit as my counselor (John 14:16)

I know the Holy Spirit as a counselor who is always with me even when sometimes I don't feel him. Knowing Him as a counselor, I never feel alone even when no one is around. The Counselor makes me feel special because He is the Spirit of God and yet loves me enough to dwell with me always. He was sent by God to comfort those who accept Him.

The Holy Spirit as my Intercessor (Romans 8:26)

The Holy Spirit as my intercessor stands in the gap for me and prays what is on my heart that agrees with what is on the heart of God. Many times, my heart is overwhelmed and I don't know what to do or what to pray for and that is when the Holy Spirit as my Intercessor steps in. There are times when the Holy Spirit steps in as my intercessor and it is with sounds of groaning, not words, coming from me.

The Holy Spirit as my Convictor of Sin (John 16:7-11)

The Holy Spirit as my convictor of sin is the One who corrects me when I am going off track or being disobedient to the instruction He has given me to do. When the Holy Spirit tells me to go pray for someone or give them a word for Him and I don't do it, then I am convicted. I know I have disappointed my Heavenly Father and that makes me very unhappy and heartbroken.

The Holy Spirit as my Guide (John 16:13)

When I think of the Holy Spirit, I think about how He leads me with decisions; a decision such as moving to Charlotte, North Carolina without having a job, a place to live, or knowing anyone. The Holy Spirit has been my guide even when it comes to picking a car or an area to live or certain items to buy. The Holy Spirit as a guide gives direction.

The Holy Spirit as my Comforter (John 15:26)

The Holy Spirit as my comforter is there to bring me peace when I am upset or confused and don't know what to do. The Holy Spirit as my comforter was there for me when my mother passed away. I had many questions for the Father about Him calling my mother home to be with Him too soon. He brought comfort by letting me know that my mother belonged to Him before she belonged to me and He shared her with me for over thirty years. The Holy Spirit also brought a young woman in my life who had her mother for only eight years so that gave me a new outlook on life and it also gave me peace.

The Holy Spirit as my Indweller (Romans 8:9-11)

The Holy Spirit as my indweller is amazing. When I think that God loves me enough that He first sent His only Son to die for my sins and then afterward, sent me the Holy Spirit to dwell in me, that just blows my mind. A Holy God sent His Holy Spirit to live on the inside of me forever. Also with the indwelling of the Holy Spirit I have the righteousness of God abiding within me.

The Holy Spirit as my Seal (2 Cor. 5:5)

The Holy Spirit as my seal is God putting a down payment on me until I return home to be with Him again. The Holy Spirit as a seal is being marked with His approval and separates me for His work. I have been chosen by God and sealed for others to see.

The Holy Spirit as my Teacher (John 14:26)

God sent the Holy Spirit to be not only my comforter but also my Teacher. The Holy Spirit as my Teacher is able to teach me all things and bring them back to my remembrance but only what I have studied. I know that if I study the word of God, the Holy Spirit promised me that He will bring it to my remembrance.

Yvonne Williams

And I will pray the Father, and he shall give you another Comforter, that he may abide with you for ever;

John 14:16

THE HOLY SPIRIT AND THE UNBELIEVER

The Holy Spirit has a work in the lives of unbelievers too. Even though He can't live within them, He uses the believers who are yielded to Him to minister to them. Remember, God's ultimate will is for us all to be saved. (John 3:16) He sent His Son to demonstrate His love in the earth that we would respond by accepting Jesus, His Blood Sacrifice, as our Savior. He uses us to preach, speak, teach, write, sing, and etc., to draw the attention of the unbelieving to Him.

John 16:8, "He will come to convict the world of sin, to show the world what has God's approval, and to convince the world that God judges it." (God's Word)

The Holy Spirit convicts the heart of the sinner. He will let them know what God approves and disapproves of. It is God's purpose that through conviction, the sinner will repent, turn from their wicked ways, and turn to Him. Unfortunately, we know that this is not always the case. In fact, many times the sinner's heart will harden and they will do more wickedly. Consider the time in Bible history when

Moses approached Pharaoh and rebuked him for enslaving the Israelites, but just as God expected, Pharaoh's heart hardened.

We have to remember this, especially as ministers, your duty to Holy Spirit is to yield Him your life that He can use you. But you don't take upon yourself the false burden of trying to save someone. Only Jesus can save. Our role is to allow Holy Spirit to govern our lives. Let Him speak to our co-workers, our parents, our children, our siblings, our neighbors, or a complete and total stranger. He just wants a chance to speak what is on the heart of God.

The Holy Spirit will tug on the hearts and minds of sinners until they come to a place of repentance but He won't force upon anyone anything they don't want.

Genesis 6:3, "And the LORD said, My spirit shall not always strive with man".

At some point, like in the very famous case of Saul, the Lord will turn His heart from a people. He wants us to repent but because He gave us the power of will, He wants our Yes to be voluntary. He is ready to forgive, love us, and make all things brand new, but the sinner man must accept that for himself.

Delisa Lindsey

I pray for them: I pray not for the world, but for them which thou hast given me; for they are thine.

John 17:9

NAMES OF HOLY SPIRIT

Convicter of Sin: (John 16:7-11) – Holy Spirit as Convicter of Sin works very well in my life. For example, if I leave the bank or work with an ink pen that doesn't belong to me, Holy Spirit will convict me and I will return it. If I say something or think something that is not right, Holy Spirit as Convicter of Sin will correct me and it is most always immediate. It is up to me to heed to Him and do what is right but that part of Holy Spirit works just fine! Even when dealing with my children, dealing with callers on my job, matters in my family, in my ministry, and at church for that matter, Holy Spirit as Convicter of Sin operates as a "motive checker" in my life – keeps me on the right path. There is an adage, "The Holy Ghost will keep you if you want to be kept", and that is true. Do not ignore what Holy Spirit is doing or saying.

Comforter/Counselor/Advocate: (Isaiah 11:2, John 14:16; 15:26; 16:7) – Holy Spirit is my Comforter in times of grief (during my grandmother's passing), in times of distress (financial crises), and in times of trials. Holy Spirit has served as Comforter by bringing back to my remembrance the Word of God to bring comfort to me.

During financial distress, He reminds me that God is a provider. There was a time of drought in my life. I was back and forth between SC and GA trying to find work and every door was closing. I was driving back from Atlanta in tears and Holy Spirit whispered to me clearly and plainly, "Have you considered my servant Job?" I cried and cried but peace overcame me and at that moment I understood what God was doing in my life.

As Counselor, Holy Spirit gives me instruction for my ministry, my household, and every area of my life. I must admit that I didn't always listen but now I ask for guidance and then wait. Holy Spirit has served as an advocate for me on my job (and sometimes it's funny to me) but someone will do or say something that causes me heartache and Holy Spirit will speak up through another on my behalf, rather it's the supervisor coming through to say that I received a compliment from a caller or kudos from another coworker. Holy Spirit also served as an Advocate for me during a time when a certain gentleman tried to destroy my character and I was told by the person the gentleman was talking to - the God in me speaks for me. In other words, I didn't have to prove anything, Holy Spirit advocated on my behalf by allowing that person to see the God in me thereby causing him to not believe what that gentleman was saying about me.

Deposit/Seal/Earnest: (2 Corinthians 1:22; 5:5: Ephesians 1:13-14) – Holy Spirit as deposit, seal, earnest or guarantee serves as my promise of my spiritual inheritance. The seal or mark of a believer is the Holy Spirit and personally I get excited when I'm speaking to someone and it's a confirmation, or they say, "Now that's the Holy Spirit because that's exactly what I needed to hear". It brings me excitement because it's a sure sign that I belong to the Father.

One day, I was sharing my testimony with a sister/friend. I called her to ask her if she would be a speaker on the conference line but I ended up sharing my testimony and before that call ended – I was in tears. I told her I didn't know why I shared that because that isn't why I called and she replied, "Sis. Marva, it was exactly what I needed to hear because for the first time in six years, I'm going through that situation". One example that I read that brought clarity to me regarding Holy Spirit as a seal/guarantee – "Holy Spirit is like the engagement ring (the promise) to me being the bride of Christ."

Intercessor: (Romans 8:26) – Holy Spirit has served as Intercessor in my life numerous times. When I don't know what to pray, sometimes I'll pray in my heavenly language. Sometimes all I can do is cry. There have been times when I have laid in bed with thoughts and I just tell God because I am numb and don't know what to do. Holy Spirit as Intercessor prays for me. I know because someone will call and minister to me or God, Himself will minister to me. I will receive peace in my spirit or my joy is restored; not always immediately but eventually. Being transparent for a moment, it probably could be immediate in most cases but sometimes not being willing to receive it. The key to Holy Spirit working and moving is giving Him permission to do so; being a willing vessel. In moments like that I have to ask for forgiveness and deliverance from pride/stubbornness.

Spirit of Revelation: (Ephesians 1:17) – Holy Spirit as Spirit of Revelation operates in my life when I get an understanding of scripture. I can read a scripture several times but when the Spirit of Revelation is alive in my spirit, I get understanding. The proof of the understanding is a changed life through application of the Word. Also you can see Spirit of Revelation in operation during Bible Study when a teacher reads the passage and several get a different revelation but each revelation is to the Glory of God. He helps each individual by being just what someone needed at that moment in life.

Marva Roseborough

DELIVERANCE

WHY WE NEED DELIVERANCE

There is so much in regards to deliverance that I was unaware of. One of the most important parts of deliverance is to know the three requirements. These are Repentance, Forgiveness, and Complete separation. I remember saying in my past days of not knowing better that I forgive, but would never forgive. I find that many people today still use such terms. This is far from true when it comes to forgiveness. When we repent and ask God for forgiveness, He does just that. We are to forgive others just as God forgives us. It is not for us to bring up that situation again. We must forgive and move forward in our lives. We must also completely separate ourselves from those things which once had us bound.

There are also ruling spirits that are operating on a daily basis in the lives of many people. An example is one who operate in Revenge, Retaliation, Anger, Violence, and Bitterness which is the prince demon of the manifestation of these spirits.

In terms of the Jezebel spirit, this spirit controls its victims. If the Jezebel spirit isn't defeated, it can and will destroy a person's life. I have been in contact with people in the past not realizing that they were operating with this spirit. I remember a few months ago, a woman requested my friendship on Facebook. After accepting the friendship, she invited me to be a guest on her Prophetic prayer line but I really wasn't interested. She messaged me once asking me to call her. Why in the world did I do that? I called the woman and she was telling me about her prayer line ministry. I told her that I wouldn't be able to join in. She further mentioned to me that they are online praying many times past midnight.

Well, needless to say, the woman went on and told me that she was going to PUSH me to get on that line! I couldn't believe what she said. I was thinking, "How in the world can you make someone do something and they've basically told you they aren't interested?" Well, I had no idea that she was operating with the spirit of Jezebel to try and get me to do what she wanted. That was the first and last time I had spoken to her. Later on, I started receiving text messages about meeting calls and the reminders about the prayer line. The woman had saved my phone number which I did not agree to become a part of any meetings. This is why we must be careful and not quick to pick up the phone with everyone. A few months later, I was invited to get in and listen on the prayer line with a guy I was in a relationship with. After listening in on the line, it didn't take me long to realize that this was the same woman who tried pushing me in on her line. She had a number of different women in on the line speaking, prophesying, and etc. I couldn't believe it, however I stayed on just to listen. There were nothing but women and the guy who invited me was the only male on the prayer line. As the prayer line was coming to a close, she opened up the line to those who wanted to sow seeds. I have no problem with sowing seeds, however we must be careful in sowing our seeds anywhere and we had better make sure that we are sowing them in GOOD ground. As she opened up the line, when someone said they would sow a seed, she also wanted to know the name of the person who spoke out. At that point, I was ready to hang up because I've never heard of such a thing. I realized later that the spirit of Jezebel was in full operation and she wanted to make sure those who said they would sow were going to actually sow because now she also had the names of each person. The guy who invited me was never told about it, but I later regretted it because he was also one who said he would sow a seed. It made me wonder what may have happened once she took everyone's name and no one was on that prayer line. Jezebel is indeed real and many of us come in contact with this spirit and we don't ever realize it.

Another spirit which is in full operation is witchcraft. Many people tend to believe that those who operate in witchcraft look like witches and mix potions every day . This is further from the truth. I realized that one of my past relationships I was involved in was witchcraft and I had no idea at the time. I was in heavy bondage during the course of the relationship. The more I wanted to break the relationship off with the guy, the more I ended up right back at the same place again. Actually the entire family had problems! His mother was a Jezebel indeed. It was her way or no way. She lied and twisted things, manipulated, and no one better not ever tell her, "No", or she would go ballistic! There were many times I didn't know who I was due to being in this relationship and I suffered from very low self esteem as a result of it. The guy was also a Mason who claimed he cut off all ties and was no longer involved, however he still had the Masonic symbol on the back of his car. I will never forget one day at his home that we got in an argument. He turned looked at me and his entire face changed while he told me that he couldn't stand me. The day he told me that was when I knew I had to get away from not only him, but his family. They were ALL crazy! The demonic spirit had manifested right before my very eyes. I cannot express to others now how we really must be careful about those we link up with and get in relationships with because this is very serious when we become involved with someone who has a spirit of witchcraft or Jezebel operating in their lives.

A few of the ways to break these curses if they have operated over our life is to live a righteous lifestyle and put on the full armor of God. We must not only pray, but the power of God should be manifested in our lives on a daily basis. We must also stay rooted in God's word. We must remove objects that can bring curses upon our lives. Many people today have objects in their homes not knowing they are curses. These can be objects hanging in our homes, worn as necklaces, or even our clothing.

It's imperative to search within ourselves to find out what it is that may be keeping us bound. Many people don't realize how generations of things in our family's history have an effect on us now. A few of the things that I have struggled with is Rejection and Bitterness. This spirit certainly stems from generations on my father's side. My father to this day still deals with Bitterness,

Unforgiveness, and Anger. There were a lot of things that happened in my father's childhood which caused him to become bitter and harbor unforgiveness. My father never dealt with these issues. These spirits eventually manifested during my childhood and even in my adult life. I had a lot of unforgiveness towards my father because of the way he treated me and especially after my mother passed away. I felt that because of the way he treated my mother in the past years, that once she became ill and passed away from cancer it was his fault. At one time my anger became so enraged that it turned into hatred for my father. My father often said many things to me which caused me much pain.

Not only did I deal with rejection from my father, but it spilled over into my relationships as well. One relationship I was in, the guy was the exact same way as my father was. I encountered much verbal abuse and jealousy from this guy. The funny thing (wasn't funny at the time), he had the same first name as my father's middle name. My heart became so wounded even recently after so much rejection, that I decided I would build a wall up so that I would not get hurt again. I felt as though I couldn't trust anyone and as a matter of fact I became very bitter all over again and said I didn't want to be bothered. After that last relationship, I became so bitter that I was ready to retaliate because I was truly sick and tired of being hurt, especially after feeling as though I'm now finally able to open up to someone I can trust. I realized I had to release the spirit of rejection and bitterness and it was time to be set free once and for all. The generational curse had to be broken!

I can say today that I thank God for being completely set free and delivered from those spirits which had me bound for years. It's important for us to realize that if we don't take control of that which is controlling us, we will continue to be bound, walk in unhealthy relationships, and will never truly be able to walk into all that God has truly called us to walk into. Thank God, I'm Free!

Jennifer Robinson

Be careful for nothing; but in every thing by prayer and supplication with thanksgiving let your requests be made known unto God.

Philippians 4:6

MAJOR DEMONIC THREATS TO KINGDOM ADVANCEMENT

I was born and raised in Rock Hill, SC. I grew up in what was considered the rural area of town and loved it. I was raised by my grandparents and the environment was happy. I mean I was so happy that I didn't realize we were economically disadvantaged until I got to college. There was so much love in our home and my grandparents raised me to reverence God. We went to church, had personal Bible Study in our home, participated in community events, and life was good and simple.

I was a Girl Scout for 11 years and traveled to many places as a child each summer for vacation. We had family gatherings regularly in our back yard with family from Baltimore, New York, and Charlotte. Life was really good. But what happened? What happened that I became distant and distrustful? What happened that I began to doubt who I was? What happened that I didn't feel good enough or worthy enough? What happened that I felt afraid? What happened that I would withdraw? Why did I become paranoid that people were always talking about me? What happened that I would make up stories about me, my family, or where I lived? Why did I become ashamed? What happened? What happened that I had the mentality of "I'm going to get you before you get me?" What happened that it became okay to be promiscuous? What happened that I began to smoke cigarettes and drink? What happened to my life with God? What happened? When did it happen and who did it?

Let's talk about how these feelings and activities can enter into a person's life, more specifically my life. Rejection is a demonic stronghold that sets out to destroy a person's life and it certainly was on course to destroy me. Rejection is an inner wound and results from a denial of love. According to thefreedictionary.com, "Rejection is the act of rejecting, reject being the root word meaning to refuse to accept, submit to, believe, or make use of. To refuse to consider or grant; deny. To refuse to recognize or give affection to (a person). To discard as defective or useless; throw away."

How do you deal with such a destructive spirit? First, you must be born again. By the saving Blood of Jesus Christ, I was made whole. I was restored by the

Blood of Jesus but the wounds and the inner hurts were still there. First step is recognizing that there is a problem; that there are some emotional and inner hurts that need to be dealt with and that there were some behaviors that had to change because they didn't compliment my new life in Christ. My mind, body, and spirit had to be renewed. The first thing after confession was forgiveness. God dealt with me on forgiving everybody who had wronged me. I had to release every hurtful relationship that I had been involved in. Some of it required conversing with some of these people. The process for me called for constant prayer and constant washing with the Word of God. I also had to undergo counseling and therapy because I had suffered years and years of hurt, pain, and wounds. Being bound by rejection even limited my relationship with God. I believed in Him but I didn't completely trust Him. Everybody else walked out on me; when would He?

I know God's word says, "He'll never leave me nor forsake me and lo, He'll be with me", but there's a difference between knowing and believing. I trusted God with some areas of my life, but not all. I wanted to totally surrender and I wanted to totally be free but rejection now had a foothold on me that after deliverance it would try to creep back in. But I have to declare that God loves me and He accepts me. I reign with Him. I am a joint heir. I am important to Him. I matter to Him. He has need of me. He has a plan and purpose for me. I am His co-worker. He adores me. He loves without conditions. He calls me friend. He delights in me. He is my Husband. He's the God, "Who sees me" and I am fearfully and wonderfully made.

For my own life, I will continue to wash with the Word, continue to pray self- examine, and to be watchful of the enemy's tactics. I will be sure I am guarded, fully armored, and be sure to not open any doors or have any cracks in my armor. In the lives of others, I share my experiences with rejection and constantly remind them of God's love for them. I minister to them through the scriptures and life experiences. I don't want to see anyone bound. The Word of God says, "He whom the Son sets free is free indeed", and it is my goal to be sure that people know this. In my ministry, I will show love to everyone, minister the Word, counsel them upon request, and pray.

In closing, as Christians we are supposed to love everyone. Be kind, be patient, be loving towards everyone you meet. You don't know what they may be dealing with and don't take offense if they don't reciprocate but pray for them and continue to show kindness (more than likely they are dealing with rejection in some form). Deal with offenses as they come, do not allow them to fester and grow. Know who you are, and forgive, forgive, and forgive.

According to studies, the absence of a father (fatherly priesthood) paves the way for a spirit of Rejection. Spirit of Rejection can enter a child from the womb based on the mind, emotions, and spirit of the mother. Rejection opens the door to rebellion. Schizophrenia begins with rejection. Sexual perversion is often engaged in to hide feelings of rejection. People suffering from rejection are usually insecure and inferior. The opposite of rejection is love. God is love.

Marva Roseborough

And these signs shall
follow them that believe;
In my name shall they cast
out devils

Mark 16:17

THREE FOLD CORD

"And though a man might prevail against him who is alone, two will withstand him. A threefold cord is not quickly broken" (Ecclesiastes 4:12). This scripture is frequently used in wedding ceremonies to describe a relationship between husband and wife with God as the center. This threefold cord is not easily broken whereas one standing alone or two standing without God may break or fall. Nelson's commentary states that this scripture is used to describe the value of friendships but this same concept can apply when talking about demonic spirits. One can work alone but with more than one that bond is not easily broken or that stronghold over one's life is not easily broken. However, it's not impossible to break. Jesus cast out demons from a man. There were so many he called himself Legion (Mark 5: 1-20).

The three fold demonic cord consists of rebellion, rejection, and a root of bitterness also known as the three R's of deliverance. These three spirits are the most prevalent and they work together to attack mankind hence forming a threefold cord. Rejection is an inner wound that directly results as a denial of love. Root of bitterness is associated with not being able to forgive. Rebellion is disobedience. If a person has been denied love at an early age possibly from neglect of one or both parents, they never forgive the parents so this root of bitterness grows and festers and as a result of already feeling unloved. Now angry and bitter, this is acted out in rebellion by disobeying God and every other authority (parents, church leaders, school teachers, supervisors, etc.). Can you see how these spirits intertwine hence forming the threefold demonic cord? I want to look closer at the spirit of rebellion as the focus of this note. I will attempt to define this spirit, give examples of what it looks like, and list the steps to be free based on personal experience.

"For rebellion is as the sin of witchcraft, and stubbornness is as iniquity and idolatry. Because thou hast rejected the word of the LORD, he hath also rejected thee from being king", (1 Samuel 15:23). According to the scripture, rebellion (not doing what God commanded) is compared to witchcraft. In other words, disobedience and rebellion is just like being a part of an occult, operating in sorcery. Sounds like serious business? It is. Don't be fooled. Rebellion is further defined in this scripture as stubbornness, pride, arrogance; becoming self-important in God's presence. Stubbornness is compared to iniquity (moral distortion and crookedness) and idolatry (worshiping objects rather than God). Rebellion is rejecting the word of God. Rejecting the word of God renounces your rightful place as king. Kingdom citizens must obey if you're going to reign in the earth. The Webster New International Dictionary defines rebellion as open resistance to, or defiance of, lawful authority.

What does rebellion look like? People who are operating under this spirit despise instruction. They are stubborn, they go out doing their own thing without submitting to authority or consulting God, they are disobedient, they are dominating, manipulative, controlling, they have a lying spirit which is a fruit of rebellion, a hardness of heart, have a hard time loving people, will not receive the truth, and seek ungodly counsel. Scriptures related to rebellion that you may want to follow up with: Proverbs 17:11, 1 Samuel 15:22-23, Proverbs 20:20, Psalm 78:8, Ezekiel 3:26, Ezekiel 12:2, Isaiah 30, Psalm 68:6, and Proverbs 29:1.

Don't overlook rebellion in your life even if you think it's simple. If your spiritual leaders ask you not to park in visitor parking spaces and you do it anyway, why? If you are not supposed to wear flip flops to work but because you work on the night shift and the managers aren't there, you wear them anyway, why? God asks you to give ten percent of your earnings and you are capable of doing so but you don't, why? God says do not commit adultery, thou shalt have no other gods before me, thou shalt not steal (this includes making copies at work without permission), why? God wants you to spread the good news of the gospel and you don't. God says you are a prophet but you won't prophesy, the speed limit is forty-five but you're traveling at a rate of sixty-five and trying to justify it because you're running late. God tells you not to marry so and so but because you love so and so you do so anyway, why? Most often we view the face of rebellion as that teen with piercings, tattoos, smoking a cigarette, disobeying parents, and continuously running away from home but it can come in the form of a robed man or woman preaching from the pulpit. Rebellion can come in the face of merely looking in the mirror!

In my own life and my experience with the threefold demonic cord because of rejection from various events in my life, I developed a root of bitterness thereby acting out in rebellion against God. Doing everything I wanted to do, I paid the cost to be boss. (Don't be fooled; God is not mocked). It is only by His grace that I'm not diseased, dead, in jail, etc. Even after I received Christ as my Lord and Savior, I was still exhibiting certain behaviors that didn't glorify God. God is so clever and sometimes comical. I was disciplining my daughter one day, I mean I was upset and I was in mid –sentence of telling her how disobedient she was that she did opposite of whatever I asked. I was really disgusted by her action and God in a gentle whisper said to me, "This is how I feel when you don't obey Me!" I fell to my face drowning in my tears. "Lord, I repent of my sins against You, Lord I never want to make You feel like I'm feeling this very moment concerning my child. Lord, forgive me for hurting You. I purpose to do Your will, not my will Lord but Your will be done in my life. I want to be a sweet smelling savor in Your nostrils." He reminded me that He would have mercy on me with everlasting kindness (Isaiah 54:8a). Now my daughter was glad that I received this chastisement from the Lord because in her bright, pretty eyes she was off the hook. But no, I had to deal with her disobedience but the manner in which I did so, the approach was different. I was able to use my encounter with God as a teachable moment with her.

There is forgiveness but there are still consequences for our actions. God led me to a book, " What Happened to

My Teen: Uncovering the Sources of Rebellion", only to find that I (directly or indirectly) was to blame for about fifty percent of my children's rebellion. Hard pill to swallow but it began to bring healing to my girls and me.

Before I close, I just want to encourage parents to find out what is going on with your children – teens specifically- if they begin to constantly rebel. Ask them questions such as, "If you could change one thing about this family what would it be? What has been taken from you that you wish you could get back? Who are you angry with right now?" Now this will not work if you have not created an atmosphere for healthy conversation in your home. (There's help for that too but that's a story for another time). But be sure to let them talk, do not respond until they're done, and do not respond without seeking the wisdom of what to say from God. And have plenty of tissue on hand because this will open the doors to uncovering what's going on with your teens and it will give you strategy for prayers and reconciliation (if there's been a rift). So parents, based on my experiences we must constantly self-examine and do not be so puffed up that we drive our children away.

In closing, I want to reiterate that the basic sin of witchcraft is rebellion against the commandments of God.

We become the enemy of God when we operate in rebellion and it is dangerous for a person to remain in rebellion. God demands to be number one in our lives and when you refuse to give Him His rightful place in your life, you are choosing an inferior god, Satan. To be free you must be honest and expose the demon; expose them to light. Overcome embarrassment and be open with God and/or the deliverance ministers. Repent - fall out of agreement with rebellion and any other evil spirits. Renunciation – turn from every sin for example if you are rebelling by indulging in wrongful sexual relationships. Watch what you look at, read, and don't even answer your phone at 1am. You already know what they want. Meditate on what God's word says concerning sexual sins. Forgiveness - in all aspects. Are you rebelling because you are harboring un-forgiveness? Put on the whole armor of God, confess positively, stay in scripture, crucify the flesh, develop a life of continuous praise and prayer, maintain a life of fellowship and spiritual ministry, and commit yourself totally to Christ. This is how to maintain your deliverance or refill your house once you're free

Marva Roseborough

And thine ears shall hear a word behind thee, saying, This is the way, walk ye in it, when ye turn to the right hand, and when ye turn to the left.

Isaiah 30:21

NEW AGE MOVEMENT: CHARISMATIC WITCHCRAFT

Witchcraft can be defined as the practice of magic especially black magic, the use of spells, and the invocation of spirits. 1 Samuel 15:23 states that rebellion is as the sin of witchcraft or divination (as some translations state). Charismatic witchcraft is witchcraft practiced in the Christian world. Charismatic Witchcraft occurs when pastors and leaders try to control their flock. Let's keep in mind that God is a gentleman and will not impose His will upon you.

Charismatic Witchcraft is usually successful on those with passive mindsets. I met a man several months ago who stated that he was a chief prophet of God. I didn't know this man's purpose for being in my life. I asked the Lord if this was possibly my husband – he quickly (thank God for speaking promptly) answered me, "No!" However, I couldn't wrap my mind around his purpose in my life. In retrospect, it is my belief that his sole purpose was to teach me a lesson on charismatic witchcraft and to be able to recognize that demon if it tries to manifest again and since I know deliverance is part of my ministry I can now help someone else.

The tell-tale signs of a person operating in charismatic witchcraft are that this person wants to control your mind. No one knows the Bible or God better than they do in their opinion. They are very inconsiderate of your time. They know how to turn on the charm to get you to do just what they want. When everything in you is screaming, "No", they have a way to make you think it's right or it's God's will. I encourage you to not doubt who you are in Christ and when your insides are churning - heed the warning. Holy Spirit is your guide and don't discount what you know just because someone claims to be chief apostle, master prophet, Right Rev. Dr. or whatever title they're claiming. Be confident in who you are.

This person constantly had a word from the Lord but later strongly suggested that I needed to sow into his ministry. When I disagreed and said that God was not leading me to sow, he would try to suggest in a roundabout way that something detrimental would happen to my children. So I would respond by prayer, "No weapons formed against me or my family shall prosper".

This person would agree with me in prayer but something still just didn't seem quite right. The light was shone upon him during a one night revival and he could no longer hide behind that title. When I confronted him, he cowered and disappeared. I spoke to my spiritual mother concerning the matter and she told me exactly what was happening, what spirit was operating, and how to pray. When I got through praying, anointing, and sanctifying my home, God showed me that this enemy was dead.

I was grateful for that experience because it showed me several things. One of those things was that because of my spiritual elevation, the evil attacks were elevating.

Other spirits operating along with Charismatic witchcraft are the Jezebel spirit and the spirit of Design. Jezebel is controlling, manipulative, and narcissistic. The spirit of Design seeks to get into the mind of a person and defile them. Charismatic witchcraft is wanting to be a spiritual "mover and shaker" without submitting to God. Again, when we don't submit to God, we are indeed rebelling and rebellion is the sin of witchcraft. Here is a prayer for those who have been on the giving and/or receiving end of this spirit.

Our Dear Heavenly and Gracious Father, please forgive us for practicing charismatic witchcraft. We forgive those who have practiced charismatic witchcraft against us. We break the power of the ruler demons over family and organizations. We break demonic ties, bonds and caps. We break soul ties to pastors, religious leaders, or any Christian who has been trying to control us. We break curses placed on us by submitting our wills to others. We break curses brought by charismatic witchcraft and control. We break the curse of Jezebel and Ahab. We renounce false gifts given by Satan. We drive out demonic works and associated spirits of witchcraft and mind control in the name of Jesus Christ. Amen.

Further Study:

1 Samuel 15:23

Exodus 22:18

Isaiah 1:2

Psalm 107:11

Ezekiel 13:6-9

www.acts17-11.com/witchcraft.html

http://www.demonbuster.com/charism2.html

Marva Roseborough

O my God, I trust in thee: let me not be ashamed, let not mine enemies triumph over me.

Psalm 25:2

REJECTION

Rejection is a serious spirit that must be handled once recognized. If not, it will eventually turn into bitterness and unforgiveness. In life, all of us at some time have faced rejection, however there are some who have faced it more than others. When one is rejected, they begin to look for others to accept them. They want to be accepted and are longing for approval. If the door continues to close on them they will eventually begin to get bitter at others, later unforgiving those who have rejected them. People truly don't realize how these spirits can tear them apart. Unforgiveness causes those who have been hurt to shut the door on others and hinders them from not trusting anyone. They may not talk about it or the experiences they have faced, but their actions speak for themselves. We have to make up in our minds that no longer will we be bound to rejection and get delivered.

From an early age I faced rejection. I was told I wasn't going to amount to much and every time I tried to fit in with others at school it didn't work. I had a very small group of friends but the majority of the time I seemed to stand alone. Dealing with so much at home and then school was a lot for me. Because of the things I had heard growing up, there were many times I believed it and thought to myself, "Yes, maybe Dad is correct". I then went into unhealthy relationships because of what I was faced with at home. The spirit of rejection had taken its course and I had no idea. Throughout my teen years and even adult years, I had harbored so much unforgiveness that I was very bitter towards my Dad. I pretty much hated him for what I had to go through as a child and how my mother had been treated. I couldn't forgive him for how I was talked to and wondered if my Dad had any feelings at all. I would often say, "I forgive but I won't forget". When people say this, they have not forgiven at all. In the course of being rejected in relationships, I soon became very bitter. It was hard to trust and I began to have the mind frame that I wanted people to just leave me alone because I was tired of being hurt over and over again.

In relocating to Charlotte, there was much rejection I faced. It took so long to find employment. I often wondered if I had made the right decision because in all my years of working I always had a steady job with no gaps ever in employment. Because of this, I became bitter. It was hard for me to go through it but even harder to see my daughter having to endure the same thing. I was ready to pack my bags on many occasions. I soon realized that the spirits I harbored are deadly and could ruin my life if I didn't take control. Deliverance from rejection is what has made me free to be all that God has called me to be and no matter what one says, does, or thinks, I must push in spite of what things look like. I thank God that I have been set free and delivered from Rejection.

Jennifer Robinson

Heal the sick, cleanse the lepers, raise the dead, cast out devils: freely ye have received, freely give.

Matthew 10:18

DEMON OF LOW SELF ESTEEM

1 Samuel 16:7 ESV, "But the Lord said to Samuel, "Do not look on his appearance or on the height of his stature, because I have rejected him. For the Lord sees not as man sees: man looks on the outward appearance, but the Lord looks on the heart."

Song of Solomon 4:7 ESV, "You are altogether beautiful, my love; there is no flaw in you."

People will look on you for what they see but don't possess the capability to see beyond what is on the surface. Saul was born in the family or tribe of Benjamin. Historically, Benjamin was considered a cursed tribe; they were small because their lewdness brought about a civil conflict among Jacob's sons that resulted in many of their male relatives being killed by their own cousins and uncles. At birth, Benjamin was cursed by his own mother, Rachel, as she lay dying while giving birth. She called him Ben Oni, son of my mourning, but Jacob intercepted the curse by renaming the infant child, Ben Jamin, son of my right hand. We can see where Saul developed his feelings of low self worth and low self esteem.

Low self esteem is a demonic spirit sent to the mouth of an individual to convince you through ridicule or other vain sayings that something is wrong with you. This demon will use them to bully you, call you out of your name, speak curses, verbally assault you to cause you to feel insignificant and worthless. It works through Hollywood to make you think you have to look like the airbrushed image on the silver screen. It works through magazines, TV, and radio as well. Low self esteem is a lie from the enemy to work against who God created you to be. You are apart of the Creation that God called Good. Whether you are fat, skinny, tall, short, black, white, poor, rich, smart or not, you were created in God's image. You are not who the enemy says you are. You are more than a conqueror through Him that loved you and you were fearfully and wonderfully made.

Thank God that even in the life of Saul, we've learned that the Lord takes many matters in consideration when He chooses for a specific work. Unfortuntaly for Saul, he could never outgrow his need to please the people. His low self esteem had actually played a pivotal role in destroying his purpose, but thanks be to God for Jesus, who won't leave us like He found us. Thank God that through the sacrificial death of Christ and His resurrection to the newness of life, we are altogether lovely and there is no flaw in us.

Delisa Lindsey

A merry heart doeth good *like* a medicine: but a broken spirit drieth the bones.

Proverbs 17:22

WOUNDED SPIRITS

Proverbs 18:14, "The spirit of a man will sustain him in sickness; but a wounded spirit who can bear?"

Psalms 109:22, "For I am poor and needy, and my heart is wounded within me."

We are spirit beings having a human experience, therefore when our spirit is wounded, it affects the way we conduct our lives and the way we interact with others. When you think about a wounded spirit being compared to a flesh wound, you think about that area being treated with ointment and bandaged to avoid physical contact which can inflict more pain. Depending on where the injury has taken place and the extent of the damage done, that wounded area may need a sling or a cast which would prohibit certain movements from taking place to facilitate speedy healing.

In terms of a person with a wounded spirit, their movements in the Kingdom need to come to a complete halt until the Balm has been applied. A wounded spirit causes a person to become fragmented and unstable. They think with their pain and they function with their pain.

Persons with wounded spirits overact to the simplest of things because their open wound renders them sensitive to what others are saying and doing. They are always watching others because their wound are still fresh and they have a fear of being hurt again.

A wounded spirit draws flies; in other words, the enemy is attracted to those whose spirits have been wounded. He uses the entrance to their spirit by way of their wound to incubate his worrisome pesty insects which feed on the person's pain. Just as a wounded person seeks medical attention, if you are wounded, seek treatment immediately from the Father. He is your balm. The psalmist makes the confession that he is poor and needy. In other words, he admits he is in need of healing.

If you are suffering from relationship wounds let the Lord apply His BALM before that putrefying sore worsens and becomes infectious. If not, when Beelzebub, Lord of the Flies gets done with you, it will carry the DNA of your wound to the next person. Get free and stay free. Stop the spread of poison in the Kingdom.

KINGDOM LIVING

LIVING THE KINGDOM MESSAGE

What must I do to understand what it means to minister the passion of Christ? What must I do to understand what it means to preach the Kingdom message? All too often Christians will spend nearly a life time void of understanding the Kingdom Message; the message of Christ. In order to understand, we must understand who we are as Kingdom citizens and we must know the mind of Christ. By the conclusion of this note, you should have an understanding of what it means to minister the passion of Christ; preaching the Kingdom message. God does not want us ignorant of His gospel message (Romans 11:25). He wants us to understand so that we don't become wise in our own eyes by following the traditions of man or what we perceive as right.

In the beginning, God created the heavens and earth. He created light, seasons, sun, moon, stars, birds, plants, fish, and every living creature including man. (Genesis 1) Specifically in Genesis 1:28, "Then God said, Let Us make man in Our image, according to Our likeness; let them have dominion over the fish of the sea, over the birds of the air, and over the cattle and over all the earth..." God has given us dominion which means HE has given us authority, control, the right to exercise control, rule, and reign over all the earth. He has given us ruler-ship or kingship meaning that you and I are kings in the earth. As kingdom citizens we rule. Who am I? Who are you in the Kingdom? We are kings. We are joint-heirs (Romans 8:17); we are ambassadors (2 Corinthians 5:20) representing the kingdom. We are part of a chosen generation, a royal priesthood (1Peter 2:9). So in knowing who we are as Kingdom citizens, as Jesus being the King of Kings (1 Timothy 6:15), as followers of Jesus, and being made in His image, we must also have His mind.

Therefore, let this mind be in you which is also in Christ Jesus. We must renew our minds daily by dying to self and strive to be Christ like. Jesus Christ served as King on earth. He healed the sick, raised the dead, made the lame walk, delivered from demons, and the Word of God says we shall do even greater works than Jesus. Jesus is love. He is giving and compassionate. He prayed. He knew who He was in the earth, exerted His power and authority, and we've been given that same power.

In conclusion, ministering the passion of Christ and living the kingdom message is proof that we understand who we are as Kingdom citizens and that we exercise our power and authority through the Blood of Jesus. We are passionate about the things of God and we understand there is more to the Kingdom of God than just being a good faithful church member. We know that God has called us each to do a work and that there are certain people assigned to us, waiting on us. We understand that we live the Kingdom. Our lives should exemplify Kingdom. We understand that we are victorious that Jesus conquered death, infirmity, poverty, fear, insecurity, addictions, religion, and everything else that comes to hinder at the grave. We do not allow our circumstances to stop us from moving forward. These things are examples of preaching the Kingdom because our lives show it. The passion of Christ is that we aren't satisfied with going to church, coming home, and going to Bible Study. We seek more, we long for more, and not just for our sakes but for the world. Passion means the sufferings of Christ, strong desire, love, fervor, zeal an intense driving, and devotedness. Ministering the passion of Christ - preaching the Kingdom message is done from the heart with a true genuine passion for God.

Lastly, in my personal life and ministry, I will apply this Kingdom mindset and live out Kingdom principles by using my gifts to enhance not only myself and my ministry but the ministry of others. I understand that Kingdom is not selfish. It is not limited but Earth should respond to me in every area as long as I am in alignment with Heaven. I understand that my presence should change the atmosphere wherever I go because that place becomes my kingdom. I will bring restoration through the power of Jesus to His people. I am a change agent through my life and ministry purposing to do my Father's will. Amen.

Marva Roseborough

And I thank Christ Jesus our Lord, who hath enabled me, for that he counted me faithful, putting me into the ministry.

1 Timothy 1 : 12

THE MORE YOU GIVE, THE MORE YOU GET...

Kingdom mathematics says the more you give the more you will get and western civilization would reply, "That just doesn't make sense." But to those of us who are Kingdom minded, we understand that the things of God does not make sense to the world. How is it that you can receive more if you give more? The word of God says, "Give, and you will receive. Your gift will return to you in full--pressed down, shaken together to make room for more, running over, and poured into your lap. The amount you give will determine the amount you get back." (Luke 6:38). We further understand this to mean that the repayment may not be monetary but comes in all forms for example, peace, joy, healing, employment, and just every need being fulfilled. Not only does Kingdom mathematics refer to giving money but it also applies to numbers or quantities in general. Let's take a look at both concepts.

Giving money is almost like a trip to the dentist. It is dreaded by most. It seems that the more we earn, the more we have to give it out but we must, as Kingdom citizens, understand that nothing we have is ours and that everything belongs to God. We understand that God loves a cheerful giver and that we should not give grudgingly but out of love. Giving should be pleasurable. We give by tithing and giving an offering unto the Lord. Kingdom citizens understand that it takes money to take care of God's house. We give from the heart and we give unto the Lord. We understand that there are blessings in sowing into the lives of others and into the ministry of others because that is assisting the advancement of the Kingdom. Our motives have to be pure in our giving just ask Ananias and Sapphira (Acts 5).

Kingdom mathematics also teaches us to not be concerned with massive numbers of people. Kingdom ministers understand that a few faithful people are more powerful than an army of unproductive people. Jesus fed the multitudes with two fish and five loaves of bread. Western civilization or a natural mind can't fathom the thought of that. I can remember as a child it always seemed we had enough no matter how little of a meal that my grandmother prepared. There was always enough for an extra plate. There was always someone stopping by and there was always enough; that's Kingdom.

Being raised in a traditional church, you would always hear the question of how many people were there and the "success" of your program depended upon how many people were present versus how many people were saved. Kingdom mathematics has taught me to not be concerned with how many people show up at my ministry events. There are certain people who ask me almost after every meeting, "How many people were there?" And if there were one or two people I would feel ashamed to answer. But if I had several people I would answer that same question with boldness and a sense of pride. Even though I understand that Kingdom work is going forth and that we ministered the word of God in our meeting, as soon as someone would ask how many people, I would feel ashamed. I know that quality is more meaningful that quantity in Kingdom ministry and success is not measured in numbers but by the fruit that my ministry is bearing. I get more joy from the praise reports as a result of something said or done through my ministry.

To make this teaching personally applicable to my life, I will no longer be ashamed of small numbers. I will appreciate where I am in my ministry and be consistent. I will be in place when the time of promotion comes. I understand that I must tithe, I do tithe, and I will continue to tithe. I believe in sowing, although it has been recently that I have pushed myself to sow more. I am stretching myself in the area of giving. My God supplies all my needs according to His riches in glory (Philippians 4:19). I will not forsake the Kingdom in my giving. Amen.

Marva Roseborough

The name of the LORD is a strong tower; the righteous run to it and are safe.

Proverbs 18:10

WHAT IS THE KINGDOM?

What is the Kingdom of God? We hear this term frequently and we even pray God's Kingdom come but what exactly is the Kingdom? The Kingdom of God is simply the rule of God; the sovereignty of God. It is demonstrating the life of Christ through our daily lives and it is Christ coming alive in us.

When we pray, "God's Kingdom come, Thy will be done on earth as it is Heaven", we are saying that everything that is going on in Heaven, everything that God is doing in Heaven, we want it right here on Earth. Kingdom understands that Christ lives in me and I have the same power and authority as He does. We are saying, "Have rule in me Jesus. Take over my life, my body". Kingdom is total surrender of your will to the will of God. "Not my will Lord but Thy will be done". Kingdom is totally removing self and operating in faith. "Lord, You said it, I believe it. You said greater works shall we do, I believe it. Instruct me and teach me in the Way". Kingdom is having such a love for people and a love for righteousness that it hurts you to see wickedness and evil.

You cry for a spirit of revival and repentance. You go the extra mile to help someone else overcome.

I have not always been Kingdom minded and have not always been productive but the good news about Jesus is that He forgives and gives us second chances. When I was truly restored – brought back – for His glory, I became good seed. Good seed produces fruit (Mark 4:20), hence my ministry was birthed. I had Bible Study and prayer with my children at home and my conduct changed. My attitude changed. I was concerned as to whether my thoughts, words, and actions were offensive to God. I am a sacrifice for other single parents; teaching them from the wounds of my pain, failures, and set-backs so that they can be healed.

Kingdom requires relationship with our Father. We can't know His will, we can't take on His mind and character if we don't know Him. This requires reading about Him in His Word, communing with Him through prayer, psalms, dance, writing, art, etc. Our worship denotes relationship. We were created to worship. We were created for God's purpose so we each have an assignment. My assignment in the earth is to preach the gospel message of Jesus Christ to the lost. When I say preach, I don't necessarily mean from a pulpit, but to "go" out to the hedges and highways. Not only to preach the gospel to a dying world but to make disciples of them. I am commissioned to spread the good news of the gospel of Jesus Christ. What do I do or what am I doing to fulfill this mandate? Clearly not enough. However, I do use social media; the World Wide Web, to spread the gospel message as well as my lifestyle. Is there more I can do? Yes. Will I do more? Yes.

"I beseech you therefore, brethren, by the mercies of God, that you present your bodies a living sacrifice, holy, acceptable to God, which is your reasonable service. And do not be conformed to this world, but be transformed by the renewing of your mind, that you may prove what is that good and acceptable and perfect will of God." (Romans 12:1-2). Kingdom is sacrifice and renewing our minds to the mind of Christ to do His perfect will. Colossians 1:28 also tells us that Christ is in us and that we are to teach men to perfection or until maturity. Therefore making disciples so they can go out. That means teaching the nations and generations. One day every knee shall bow and every tongue will confess that Jesus is Lord. The harvest is plentiful. I will do my part, will you?

In closing, I want to share these words after hearing a teaching on the Kingdom of God. I was bending down in my closet searching for a shoe and I could actually feel my heartbeat change patterns. It was not heartburn or palpitations. I've experienced both and this was different. I knew that God was performing some type of procedure on my heart. Later in my quiet time He gave me these words:

The rhythm of my heartbeat is changing. Father, I know it's You fine tuning what you've placed inside of me. Yes Sir, I know it's true. Yesterday's pain and failure has moved out of the way; my heart is beating to a new rhythm this day. Created in Your image – but strayed from the course – my heartbeat became out of sync with each sin, act of disobedience, iniquity but because You love me and allowed me to find my way, You called me back to You and I'll worship You always. I feel my heartbeat changing and all I can understand is that You've changed it back to its original state as in Your original plan. The prodigal daughter has returned, taking her rightful place. Thank You Lord, for it was only by Your saving grace. The rhythm of my heartbeat is changing; Father I know it's You. Back to its original design; created in the image of You.

Your heart has to resemble His heart and if you yield yourself and yield your body, He will do it. What is the Kingdom? "It is the heartbeat of Christ".

Marva Roseborough

And the peace of God, which passeth all understanding, shall keep your hearts and minds through Christ Jesus.

Philippians 4:7

KINGDOM LEADERS

Go ye therefore and preach the gospel within the confines of your church building. Raise up a body of pew warmers, flamboyant choir directors, sleeping deacons, mean ushers, stingy kitchen/hospitality crew who keep all the good Macaroni and Cheese for themselves, missionary boards 1, 2, and 3 who never go overseas or do any local missionary work, sell raffle tickets, and have choir anniversaries to see who sings the best. This is the gospel according to Church Leadership. Church leadership says you have to have a title and the more titles you have, "Rt. Rev. Dr. Dew Good, Sr.", the more successful you are. Church Leadership says you take communion on the first Sunday of each month and you must wear white if you serve on the Deacon/Deaconess Board. Church Leaders are only leaders on Sunday mornings, Wednesday nights, and special church occasions. Church Leadership does not teach that everyone has a ministry and church leadership does not groom you and push you past ushering, singing on the back row of the choir, or serving cookies and Kool-Aid at Vacation Bible School. Church Leadership is self-promoting and is concerned with numbers, large buildings, and making sure that the high tithers are satisfied and pacified. Is God pleased with this gospel? How can I change? How can I transition from this state? This is all I have known.

It is unfortunate that we have been bound by traditions and religion but Jesus came to set the captives free and whom the Son sets free is free indeed. At the point of salvation, we became joint-heirs with Christ; adopted in the royal family therefore making us kings. As kings, we are all leaders and are all called to serve in various capacities. Wherever we are, whether it is at home, work, church, PTO, or school, we understand that we are leaders. We glorify and exemplify Christ everywhere, every day, and in every area of our lives not just when the doors of the church are open. Some Kingdom leaders may have titles and some may not and we are not offended by it because we understand our place. Kingdom leaders edify the Body of Christ; helping to train and equip believers. Kingdom leaders are not confined to the four walls of the church. Kingdom leaders understand the Gospel according to Jesus Christ. "Go ye therefore and make disciples of all nations, baptizing them in the name of the Father, and of the Son, and of the Holy Spirit, teaching them to observe all things that I have commanded you..." (Matthew 28:19-20). With the measure of faith that we have each been given, we do what is within our reach to "go". Kingdom leaders regard their character and walk upright. Kingdom leaders strive for holiness and understand that they are sanctified; set apart. Kingdom leaders truly eat, breathe, and live the word. The word says, "Owe no man anything but love", and in that regard, Kingdom leaders become debt free. The Bible says to obey those placed in authority over you. We submit to leadership on the job, at church, and in our homes. We seek God to know who we are and how we can best serve Him to advance the Kingdom. Kingdom leaders love what they do for God without looking for recognition. Kingdom leaders do not wait until they have "arrived" before teaching and preaching the gospel. They use what resources are available. Kingdom leaders reach out to all regardless of sex, race, religion, and socio-economic status. Kingdom leaders are equal opportunists and take advantage of every open door for Kingdom advancement. Kingdom leaders are self-less.

How do I know I am a Kingdom leader? I never fit in with the politics of church leadership. I have always felt in my heart there was more to God beyond what I was seeing in church. I have a strong desire to see people delivered, healed, set free from emotional bondage and every form of bondage. In my personal life and ministry, I will continue to seek God, continue to become trained and equipped, not to attach some initials to my name, but to "Go ye therefore" and advance the Kingdom. The rhythm of my heart beat is changing. Amen.

Marva Roseborough

Great peace have they which love thy law: and nothing shall offend them.

Psalm 119:165

TRANSITIONING IN MINISTRY

We, as people of God, have to realize that there is power in the name of Jesus. There is power in prayer, worshiping, and fasting. In the carnal mind, we may think we always need to call on the pastor to get our break through or to get a prayer though. We have the same authority as them as the same way that God gave them power. He has given power to all of His kings. While it is true that some people have more authority when using their power but as a Kingdom leader, you have the Spirit of God that dwells in you that causes demonic spirits to become subject to you. This is not a license to go anywhere you want and do whatever you want, you still have to submit to the kings over various kingdoms that already exist such as schools, employment, and the law enforcement. Know your power but don't be carnal and foolish, let the Spirit of God guide you.

As a Kingdom minister, your ministry doesn't stop in your own race (color). It expands when you mature into becoming a colorblind minister. It's not all about saving one specific race. When working outside of the four walls you have to realize that one, everyone will not look alike and two, not everyone learns the same way. You as a man or woman of God have to know how to connect with people of different nationalities as well as different personalities.

It is important to know which spirits you are up against when ministering in church and outside of church. You have to come to terms with realizing that some people have situations which happened to them in their past where certain spirits attached themselves to them. Prophesying and laying hands only goes but so far. The people must be taught how to deal with certain spirits. It doesn't matter how many times you prophesy someone a new car, if they have demons manifesting around their thoughts and confusing them 24 hours a day, then what you have is a blessed and possessed situation. They receive the car you released but you forgot to deal with that mind battling spirit using them. When we are training disciples, we have to put down our flesh and let the Kingdom man rise up. If we are jealous of how fast these persons are learning or worried about them passing us in ministry, then first of all, we need to repent for being selfish, and secondly, you have made it difficult for them to get to the place they need to be because we are trying to keep them below their assignment.

We as Kingdom leaders can also begin to teach our brethren how to survive the worldly system. Teaching them how to save money, how to invest, and how to plan are just only a couple of things we can do for each other outside of the four walls of the church. Everything about us must become Kingdom and if our brothers and sisters in the Lord don't know how to manage a certain area in their life, why shall we not help them and share some of our knowledge in the area they need help in? It is important that we not be selfish with our knowledge.

It is also important that we remain steadfast in the Word of God. The deeper we are in our relationship with God, the more strategies and understanding we will have for how to minister to certain crowds. We must understand that we must put in work to receive the reward. If we are just waiting on everything to be handed to us after it's prophesied then God may not move. Yes of course, He can, but He may not because we are not giving Him anything to work with. For God to work in our lives, we have to give God something to work with. We have to come into partnership with God whether it is worshiping, tithing, ushering or whatever you "do " for God. The key words in that last sentence is, "Do for God". When we do for God and come into agreement with His will full heartily, He has no problems moving on your behalf.

Tystaytian Holloway

Peace I leave with you, my peace I give unto you: not as the world giveth, give I unto you. Let not your heart be troubled, neither let it be afraid.

John 14:27

KINGDOM BALANCE

Jesus taught His disciples to follow His principles, not just His person. I grew up in church. I heard a lot about traditions, religion, and emotions but very little about the principles of Jesus. It seemed like Christians struggle between the two, the person of Jesus and the principles of Jesus but they work hand-in-hand. Some believers elaborate more the importance of the Spirit above the Word while others exalt the Word above the Spirit. What happens when someone misses knowing the person of Jesus Christ? "Many will say to me in that day, Lord? Lord? Have we not prophesied in thy name? And in thy name have cast out devils? And in thy name done many wonderful works? And then will I profess unto them, I never knew you: depart from me, ye that work iniquity". (Matthew 7:22-23) Likewise, missing the principles can result in some serious consequences too. "He that rejecteth me, and receiveth not my words, hath one that judgeth him: the word that I have spoken, the same shall judge him in the last day". (John 12:48)

There are Godly men and women walking in righteousness and true holiness, knowing the person of

Jesus, but they are poverty stricken. On the other hand, there are sinners who laugh at Christians. They know the principles of God and they walk in prosperity and health but they do not know the person of Jesus Christ. The wealth of the sinners will not completely come to us if we just know the person of Jesus. Coming from a word perspective, some would rather have the person of Jesus Christ than the principles, but being children of God means we do not have to choose which one we get because we can have them both. While it is true, salvation is a personal relationship with Jesus Christ, however, there is another side to this relationship that cannot be ignored. The other side of the Person of Jesus is the Principles of Jesus. We need to focus on both sides of our walk with the Lord: the person of Jesus Christ and His principles. We do not need to be "religious" and choose one or the other. We must be radical on both sides of the scale and build both of them faithfully, if we are going to be balanced.

Avery Ascue

But flee from these things, you man of God, and pursue righteousness, godliness, faith, love, perseverance and gentleness.

1 Timothy 6:11

CALLED TO MINISTRY

Having a 'calling' and fulfilling the calling are two very different things. We all are called to be disciples of the Lord Jesus. Some receive more responsibility with their callings because they have proven themselves worthy of being capable of such. (Luke 12:48, Eph. 4:1) Some are more yielded than others, some are more honorable vessels than others so rightly, the Lord bestows upon them more weight but He still has no respect of persons but for the one holding an index card claiming they have been called, when are you planning on fulfilling that call? How many times does the Lord have to call you? Why does He have to send twenty prophets to give you the same word? What is wrong with your understanding? The Lord called His disciples, one time! Elijah called Elisha, one time! What makes us think we are so special that He has to keep ringing our number because no one is answering the call?

Further, just because you are called does not mean you need to make up business cards and grab a passport! All of those who are called are not being sent to the nations. If your assignment is to the children in your back yard, that is your prophetic assignment to mentor them, pray for them and see them through to college. That assignment, dear friend, is just as important in the Kingdom of God as the one holding revivals of 10,000 people. Obedience is obedience in all flavors.

Since the Lord has called you, rid yourself of your excuses, step down from the your seat of do nothing, and do what the Lord 'called' you to do! God has made us every intelligent therefore we need not be told the same thing every day. Be obedient, submit yourself, cut your carnal ties until you have the strength to deal with them without being influenced by them and go on to Glory.

There is a custom among the believing ones to holler, "Confirmation", when we have heard the same word God repeated. But truth be told, when the Lord has to repeat His instructions to us, we need to make sure the 'confirmation' is not proof of our rebellion for not hearing the Lord the first time. Some of those 'confirmations' may just very well be a 'rebuke' in disguise and in those cases we need to repent of being disobedient and slothful.

Delisa Lindsey

PROPHETIC MINISTRY

UNDERSTANDING PROPHETIC PEOPLE

One awesome value of prophetic people is the level of intimacy we have with our Heavenly Father. This is a place many other prophetic people and I can go beyond the veil and enter into God's holy chambers. This is a place we all should embrace and never want to leave.

The dimension of prophetic that suits me is prophetic ministry of dance. I thank God for allowing the Holy Spirit to be the grantor of spiritual gifts. This gift grants me the ability to minister to God's people in areas such as worship, warfare, praise, encouragement, as well as the spirit of creativity.

One is born into the office of the prophet. The gift of prophecy is just that, a gift It may just be for one given time and never used again. The spirit of the prophetic is the flow of the Holy Spirit as He is moving from person to person. All these are relevant today because God shows up in the areas He chooses just as He did in former seasons.

When it comes to hindrances of the prophetic, mine is one of fear. Anyone who call themselves a prophet and does not take heed to consecrate themselves on a regular basis is walking a thin line. Prophets are accountable for what comes out of their mouths. A true prophet will only speak the Word of God.

To be successful in the prophetic, one must stay in God's face every day. It takes intimacy to be in that place to hear from God. We have to stay on our face and in doing this, the doors of true commuinication are open for God to speak through His prophets what, "Thus says the Lord".

The type of prophet that appeals most to me is the "Miracle Working Prophet". Why? Because I want to experience wonders, signs, and miracles taking place in the people of God's life. I want to see the dead raised, the blind to see, and the sick healed.

What is prophecy? Prophecy is God's divine endowment and measure of grace to speak His mind, will, counsel, and purpose in one's life through the instrumentality of yielded vessels as led by the Spirit of the Lord. Prophecy has to line up with the Word of God! If it does not, you better pass that on by. It has to line up with God's living Word!!!

Virginia Holt

For God hath not given us the spirit of fear; but of power, and of love, and of a sound mind.

2 Timothy 1:7

PROPHETIC PEOPLE

Prophetic people are intercessors born to intercede for the nation. Prophetic people are constantly in prayer and they live a lifestyle interceding for people as well. As a prophetic person, one can't have a sluggish prayer life. They are to be alert and watchful of the things going on in the world. A prophetic person is not just in intercession for themselves, they also live a lifestyle of fasting. An intimate relationship with God is imperative for prophetic people.

The prophetic presbytery is interested in seeing others birth their visions, calling, and destiny. They want people to know that they have a purpose and not just sit idly doing nothing in life. Many people don't know the potential they have and I want to push them to get into that place of envisioning and fulfilling the call of God for their life.

Tapping into the prophetic, I have been able to discern spirits now more than before which has come from spending more alone time with God. I also have a burden to see people healed. For me, this goes just beyond praying for them. I want to see the glory of God healing individuals just as the apostles did in Acts. I have noticed many times when praying for others or calling out certain illnesses in prayer that I get a tingling sensation in my hands which has increased over the months even in times when I'm not in prayer. I sit closely and spend time not just talking but listening to hear from God. There are many things that I see and hear as well in the spiritual realm.

I feel that the biggest misconception people have about the prophetic is thinking that just because they have spoken to someone or confirmed something that they are now walking in the office of a Prophet. I have had many get excited because they have heard that there is an awesome prophet coming to town. One example I remember is someone telling me about a prophet coming here and that he was accurate in knowing names, addresses, etc. Well it did not faze me then when I was told this and it still does not now. I have learned that one may think this person is a prophet, however they are just operating in the gift of knowledge at that time.

There are many in the prophetic who are unwilling to develop their character. They do not want to submit and they want to do things their way. This is very dangerous because when a person becomes prideful, they refuse to hear correction and end up acting out of the spirit of rebellion. No one can expect to do things their way and be successful in any part of ministry. If one has a shallow foundation of the Word of God and won't get in the Word of God by diligently studying and obeying, they won't be able to submit to others because they cannot be obedient to God first.

One must not only read the word, but study. One can't have a lack of the Word of God within themselves and truly expect to move forward. The flesh must be crucified daily, not sometimes, which means we must live a lifestyle of fasting. When interceding, we must go above our own prayers. Intercession is not about us so we must make sure our prayers don't become selfish.

Prophecy is speaking boldly by the will of God. Worshipping and speaking to yourself in song is also a part of prophecy. The last song the Holy Spirit placed inside of me was, "Flow to You".

There are a few experiences in which I have seen others lack prophetic protocol. At my former church, I noticed once that when one person gave a word there were others who appeared to be competitive. I have seen many times where others will share every vision and dream they have had. There is a time and season to everything and I know that every dream and vision is not to be shared with others. Many, I feel, do this just to be seen and have others feel as if they know something. There were many times I have had visions and dreams, even in church seeing angels for example. But instead of getting up, I chose to be quiet. Sometimes I have wanted to share a vision with someone but I know that I couldn't. It's imperative that protocol is followed and we know how to stay in our lane.

With personal prophecy we must adhere and align ourselves with the Word of God. We must also have faith in order for the prophecy to be fulfilled. I have found many want a Word but they don't want to meet the conditions of what it takes for that prophecy to become manifested in their life.

Jennifer Robinson

Casting all your care upon him; for he careth for you.

1 Peter 5:7

THE PROPHETIC PAUSE

Revelation 8:1 NLT, "There was silence throughout heaven for about half an hour."

Acts 5:7, "And it was about the space of three hours after, when his wife, not knowing what was done, came in."

Pay attention to time intervals. Notice when God is moving real strong in your life and those times when it seems as if He has taken a 'leave of absence'. The Lord is Spirit and He is always moving but because our spirits are cased in human flesh, if we don't naturally see a thing moving, we determine that it isn't. It's those times when our Father is silent that we really need to pay attention to. When He is silent, Heaven is moving.

In the very heat of His trial, Jesus asked the question, "Father, why have You forsaken Me?" Notice that there was silence but notice also that moments thereafter the sky darkened and the earth began to quake. When you sense that Prophetic Pause, know that something is amiss and that God is about to do something remarkable and unfathomable in your life.

As the Lord plans the next move to take place in your life, there will be what is called a 'prophetic pause'.

Things will get quiet in the spirit realm. Remember what happened with Daniel? He thought that the Lord did not hear his prayers but that was not the case. Heaven heard his prayers but there was a prophetic pause because the enemy had to be restrained that Daniel's answer could be released. During this 'pause', take the time to reflect and introspect. This is where you assess where you are, what you have, and what you need to function in the next place. Use that time wisely because it may just bring the moment of rest you will need to prepare for what is to come.

Consider our four seasons, winter, spring, summer, and fall. Fall interrupts Summer with a pause before Winter as a climate controller preparing for what is to come. When it seems to you as if the season has paused and things aren't progressing as you think they should, use that space of time for preparation. Think about it as the space between contractions when a woman is in labor to give birth. She uses that time to sip ice, find a comfortable position, and collaborate with nurses. You must do the same in your prophetic pause, sip while you can, breathe, relax, and contemplate strategies for what is about to take place.

Delisa Lindsey

For God so loved the world, that he gave his only begotten Son, that whosoever believeth in him should not perish, but have everlasting life.

John 3:16

THE PROPHETIC MINISTRY

Prophetic people must have an intimate relationship with God. God states in His Word in Revelation 4:11 that, "All things were created by Him and for His pleasure they were created." When someone becomes intimate with God, that person starts to learn His character and His heart. You will also learn what brings God pleasure and will strive to do those things.

Prophetic prayer contains a Word of Wisdom and Knowledge which reveals the mind of God. The Word of God says in Romans 8:26, "That the Spirit of God helps our infirmities for we know not what we should pray for as we ought: but the Spirit itself maketh intercession for us with groanings". That scripture confirms that no one really knows how to pray correctly. Being a willing vessel and an instrument that God can use allows Jesus, the Chief Intercessor, to pray to the Father on our behalf which brings God glory.

I love to watch and be a part of how the prophetic ministry flows. The anointing will begin to flow through the musicians who play skillfully, then the anointing will flow through the singers, then flows through the dancers in worship as God gives someone a prophetic revelation, and then the prophets will grab hold and begin to prophecy to individuals one by one under God's heavy anointing. It is just awesome to watch and be a part of that atmosphere. I have been a part of many ministries during my life time but my soul has not experienced the fullest of prophetic ministry until I became a part of True Love Church of Refuge and God allowed me to see the prophetic ministry all flow together. Now, I cannot imagine service any other way.

The Spirit of prophecy is neither a gift nor an office but an anointing and usually happens during worship or as God pleases. The Gift of prophecy is found in the Holy Spirit. It dwells in the Holy Spirit and is also known as a descending gift. The office of the prophet is for those individuals born a prophet who continuously reveal the voice, counsel, mind, will, and eternal purpose of God. It is shown with signs, wonders, and manifestations following them. All three are relevant today because God can and desires to use all three. There are times when God choses to use the Gift of prophecy, which dwells in the Holy Spirit which all believers should have. Then there are other times when God allows someone to walk in the Spirit of prophecy for one service but then He calls His prophet that He continues to reveal His heart too.

I believe one of the greatest hindrances in the prophetic is the refusal to yield and submit. The Word of God teaches that obedience is better than sacrifices and that disobedience is like witchcraft. When you refuse to yield and submit to your leaders, you are refusing to yield and submit to God. When you can't yield and submit, you become un-teachable and you hinder your growth and development in God.

One who flows in the prophetic successfully is one who has an intense personal and corporate worship with the Father regularly and consistently. One cannot successfully flow in the prophetic if they are not consistently communing with Father on a daily or sometimes hourly basis. You must be willing to spend great amounts of time with God to tap into His heart.

Prophecy is God's divine endowment and measure of grace to speak His mind, will, counsel, and purpose in one's life through His yielded vessels. It is the speaking forth boldly the authority of the Word as quickened by the Spirit. Prophecy does not make you a prophet.

I have been at a service when God used someone in tongues and someone or I should say more than one came after to give the explanation but was almost fighting to get the microphone to speak! All I could do was shake my head because I know that God is not the author of confusion and that is exactly what that was. I have also witnessed a prophet who acts as if there can only be one prophet in the house unless they happen to being visiting but two prophets cannot dwell in the same house!

The fundamentals of a personal prophecy is conditional such as; are you meeting the conditions of your prophecy? Prophecy is in part realm and is not perfection. Prophecy requires faith on the part of the individual receiving the prophecy. All prophecy is to agree with the written Word of God and never to be used to take away or substitute the Word of God. Prophecy is never to substitute spiritual authority. The chief motivation of prophecy is the love of God.

Yvonne Williams

Prayer for Salvation

Dear God in heaven, I come to you in the name of Jesus. I acknowledge to You that I am a sinner, and I am sorry for my sins and the life that I have lived; I need your forgiveness.

I believe that your only begotten Son Jesus Christ shed His precious blood on the cross at Calvary and died for my sins, and I am now willing to turn from my sin.

You said in Your Holy Word, Romans 10:9 that if we confess the Lord our God and believe in our hearts that God raised Jesus from the dead, we shall be saved.

Right now I confess Jesus as the Lord of my soul. With my heart, I believe that God raised Jesus from the dead. This very moment I accept Jesus Christ as my own personal Savior and according to His Word, right now I am saved.

Thank you Jesus for your unlimited grace which has saved me from my sins. I thank you Jesus that your grace never leads to license, but rather it always leads to repentance. Therefore Lord Jesus transform my life so that I may bring glory and honor to you alone and not to myself.

Thank you Jesus for dying for me and giving me eternal life.

Amen.

MEET THE CONTRIBUTORS

John Lindsey
Apostle and Overseer,
Author of "Stand Up:
Be A Real Man"

Delisa Lindsey
Prophet and Overseer,
Publisher and Author,
"Displacing Demonic
Gate Watchers"

Yvonne Williams
Pastor and Author,
"Religion to Relationship"

Marva Roseborough
Evangelist and Author,
"Is He the One?"

Jennifer Robinson

Prophet and Author,

"Purpose Beyond the Pain"

Avery Ascue

Author,

"12 Keys to Restoring America"

Shelia Johnson

Evangelist, Head of Hospitality

Virginia Holt

Prophet, Head of Prophetic

Fire Dance Ministry

Coviel Holloway

Deacon

39573598R00081

Made in the USA
Charleston, SC
12 March 2015